SMALL KITCHENS
PETITES CUISINES
KLEINE KÜCHEN

EVERGREEN

EVERGREEN is an imprint of

Taschen GmbH

© 2005 TASCHEN GmbH

Hohenzollernring 53, D-50672 Köln

www.taschen.com

Editor Editrice Redakteur:
Simone Schleifer

English translation Traduction anglaise Englische Übersetzung:
Nadja Leonard

French translation Traduction française Französische Übersetzung:
Marion Westerhoff

Proof reading Relecture Korrektur lesen:
Matthew Clarke, Marie-Pierre Santamarina, Anja Llorella Oriol

Art director Direction artistique Art Direktor:
Mireia Casanovas Soley

Graphic design and layout Mise en page et maquette Graphische Gestaltung und Layout:
Diego González

Printed by Imprimé par Gedruckt durch:
Anman Gràfiques del Vallès, Spain

ISBN: 3-8228-4174-9

Contents
Index
Inhalt

Introduction
Introduction
Einleitung

Cooking means much more than the simple preparation of meals. Recipes, ingredients and cooking styles from all over the world have substantially expanded the gastronomic repertoire and have also influenced cooking and eating habits.

Today's kitchen must satisfy a variety of functions, which means that the requirements in this area are dependent on the particular family setup and space available, to a far greater extent than in any room in the house.

Depending on lifestyle or the occasion, the kitchen can be the center for cooking and eating or simply a comfortable place space for the family to meet. In households in which cooking is not an obligation but is primarily regarded as a hobby, the kitchen's aesthetic appearance is of a fundamental importance. In other cases, however, the look of a kitchen is determined by the combination of freezer, refrigerator and microwave, as teh user is mainly interestedin heating up precooked meals as quickly and practically as possible.

The wide range of individual requirements has led to a great diversity in the kitchens on the market. They range from open kitchens integrated into the living area to panorama kitchens with an excellent view of the surroundings, from self-contained units to large family kitchens.

The planning and design of a kitchen is dependent on the layout and organization of the various elements and a careful selection of materials, wich are found in a huge range of colors, structures and surface treatments, providing possibilities of diverse combinations and choices. Stainless steel, wood, marble, glass and synthetic materials are the most frequently used materials. Often they offer the highest levels of functionality in the form of a tastefully appointed mix of materials.

Technical innovations in the field of cookers, refrigerators and other kitchen appliances have greatly enhanced cooking from both an ergonomic and economic point of view. With regard to design, there is a trend to replace built-in kitchens in favor of individual elements. Examples of this are the free-standing refrigerator with stainless steel coating or the extractor hoods, which are no longer integrated into the furniture, but rather decorate the kitchen as independent design objects.

Small Kitchens offers ideas, a wealth of contemporary kitchen design which take into account limitations in space while also satisfying today's residential requirements. Leading designers, architects and manufacturers show that it is entirely possible to unite functionality and aesthetics with a small area.

Faire la cuisine va au-delà de la simple préparation de plats. Recettes, ingrédients et cuisines du monde entier ont élargi le répertoire culinaire, influençant ainsi les habitudes et l'art de la table.

La cuisine d'aujourd'hui, déclinant une multitude de fonctions, définit des exigences qui dépendent de chaque structure familiale et de la place disponible, complètement différentes des autres pièces de la maison.

Au gré du style de vie ou de l'occasion, la cuisine peut devenir un centre où l'on cuisine et prend les repas ou tout simplement un coin sympathique où la famille se retrouve. Dans les ménages où faire la cuisine n'est pas une obligation mais surtout un passe-temps, l'esthétique de la pièce a la part belle. Citons enfin les cuisines dont l'apparence est déterminée par l'association réfrigérateur, congélateur et micro-onde. Ici, l'utilisateur est surtout intéressé par le réchauffement pratique et rapide de plats pré cuisinés.

La multiplicité des besoins et exigences individuelles de l'utilisateur engendre une grande diversité de modèles de cuisine allant des cuisines ouvertes, intégrées dans la pièce à vivre, aux cuisines panoramiques, dotées d'une vue splendide sur les environs, en passant par les îlots de cuisine et les grandes cuisines familiales. Le style choisi met en avant la personnalité et les goûts individuels de l'utilisateur.

La planification et la conception de la cuisine dépendent de la distribution et de l'organisation des éléments de cuisine et du choix judicieux des matériaux. La grande diversité d'aspect de ces derniers, que ce soit au niveau des couleurs, structures et traitements de la surface, offre à l'utilisateur une multitude de combinaisons et de choix. Acier inoxydable, bois, marbre, verre et matières synthétiques sont les matériaux les plus souvent employés dont le mélange de très bon goût est souvent allié à une fonctionnalité exceptionnelle.

Les innovations techniques au niveau des fours, réfrigérateurs et autres appareils de cuisine ont permis l'optimisation des activités culinaires, tant sur le plan ergonomique qu'économique. Quant au design, la tendance actuelle dans ce secteur délaisse les cuisines intégrées en faveur d'éléments individuels modulables. Citons l'exemple du réfrigérateur indépendant habillé d'acier inoxydable ou la hotte aspirante, qui ne sont plus encastrés dans le mur, mais devenus objets de design, ils décorent la cuisine.

L'ouvrage *Petites cuisines* est une mine d'or d'idées au service de l'agencement contemporain de la cuisine, qui, tenant compte de la réduction de l'espace, sont à l'aune des critères d'habitat actuels. Designers, architectes et fabricants de grande renommée nous montrent qu'il est parfaitement possible de réunir fonctionnalité et esthétique au sein d'un petit espace.

Kochen bedeutet weitaus mehr als die bloße Zubereitung von Speisen. Rezepte, Zutaten und Kochstile aus der ganzen Welt haben das Repertoire der Küche enorm erweitert und damit auch Einfluss auf die Koch- und Essgewohnheiten genommen.

Die Küche von heute hat eine Vielzahl unterschiedlicher Funktionen zu erfüllen, was zur Folge hat, dass die Anforderungen an diesen Ort in Abhängigkeit der jeweiligen Haushaltsstruktur und der vorhandenen Fläche so verschieden sind wie an kaum einen anderen Raum des Hauses.

Je nach Lebensstil und Anlass kann die Küche entweder zum Zentrum für Kochen und Essen werden oder auch einfach nur dem gemütlichen Zusammensitzen der Familie dienen. In Haushalten, in denen keine Verpflichtung besteht, kochen zu müssen und Kochen vorwiegend als Hobby betrachtet wird, steht hingegen die ästhetische Komponente des Raumes mehr im Vordergrund. Schließlich sind auch die Küchen zu nennen, in welchen Kühl-Gefrierkombinationen und Mikrowellengeräte das Bild bestimmen. Hier geht es vor allem um das praktische und schnelle Aufwärmen von Fertiggerichten.

So unterschiedlich wie die individuellen Ansprüche und Bedürfnisse der Benutzer sind, so verschieden sind auch die angebotenen Küchenmodelle. Sie reichen von offenen, in den Wohnraum integrierten Küchen, über Kochinseln und Wohnküchen bis hin zu Panorama-Küchen, die eine exzellente Aussicht auf die Umgebung ermöglichen. Verschiedene Stilrichtungen betonen darüber hinaus die Persönlichkeit und den individuellen Geschmack jedes Einzelnen.

Bei der Küchenplanung und -gestaltung kommt es neben der Aufteilung und Anordnung des Kücheninventars auch auf eine durchdachte Auswahl der Materialien an. Diese weisen in Bezug auf Aspekte wie Farbe, Oberflächenbeschaffenheit und Verarbeitung große Unterscheide auf und erlauben somit zahlreiche Kombinations- und Wahlmöglichkeiten. Edelstahl, Holz, Marmor, Glas und Kunststoffe sind die am häufigsten verwendeter Werkstoffe. Oftmals erfüllen sie in Form eines geschmackvoll abgestimmten Materialmixes den Anspruch höchster Funktionalität.

Technische Innovationen auf dem Gebiet der Herde, Kühlschränke und anderer Küchengeräte haben dafür gesorgt, dass die Tätigkeiten in der Küche sowohl unter ergonomischen als auch unter ökonomischen Gesichtspunkten optimiert wurden. Was das Design betrifft, zeichnet sich auf diesem Gebiet ein Trend weg von Einbaugeräten und hin zu Einzelelementen ab. Beispiele wären der freistehende Kühlschrank mit Edelstahlverkleidung oder die Dunstabzugshaube, die nicht mehr in die Möbel integriert ist, sondern als unabhängiges Designobjekt die Küche dekoriert.

In *Kleine Küchen* werden Ideen und Anregungen für eine zeitgemäße Küchengestaltung geboten, die unter Berücksichtigung einer begrenzten Nutzfläche repräsentativ für die heutigen Wohnbedingungen sind. Annerkannte Designer und Architekten sowie renomierte Hersteller zeigen, dass es durchaus möglich ist, Funktionalität und Ästhetik zu vereinen und auf einer kleinen Nutzfläche umzusetzen.

Design Aspects
Critères de design
Designaspekte

The layout of the room, as well as the choice between an integrated or enclosed kitchen, between a self-contained unit or a eat-in kitchen, are the first parameters to consider determining the style or design of this space. Then, through the selection of various materials, design aspects can be more precisely defined, taking into account nowadays both their functionality and visual appeal. By using appropriately selected colors, space problems can be ingeniously hidden and various shades can interact to create a variety of effects in combination with lighting. In general, bright colors and the use of assorted materials are recommended for small spaces.

La distribution de la pièce et le choix d'une cuisine intégrée ou fermée, d'un îlot de cuisine ou d'une cuisine-coin repas, sont les premiers paramètres à considérer dans la détermination du style et de l'agencement de cet espace de vie. Ensuite, le choix de divers matériaux pourra mieux définir les critères de design qui, de nos jours, doivent réunir les exigences accrues de fonctionnalité et d'esthétique. L'emploi de couleurs bien choisies peut masquer certains problèmes de place et de surcroît, sous l'effet de la lumière les diverses tonalités peuvent aussi créer divers effets. A petits espaces correspondent en général des couleurs vives et l'emploi de matériaux assortis.

Die Aufteilung des Raumes sowie die Entscheidung, ob eine in den Raum integrierte oder geschlossene Küche, eine Küchenzeile oder eine Essküche gewünscht wird, sind die ersten Schritte, wenn es darum geht den Stil und eine Gestaltungsrichtung festzulegen. Anschließend können durch die Wahl verschiedener Materialien die Designaspekte genauer definiert werden. Diese müssen neben ihrer Funktionalität heutzutage auch den Anspruch hoher Ästhetik erfüllen. Durch den Einsatz adäquat ausgewählter Farben können Platzprobleme dezent kaschiert werden, wobei die verschiedenen Farbtöne im Zusammenspiel mit Licht wiederum unterschiedliche Effekte erzeugen. Bei kleinen Räumen sind generell helle und leuchtende Farben, sowie die Verwendung dazu passender Materialien zu empfehlen.

Distribution
Distribution
Aufteilung

Lighting
Eclairage
Beleuchtung

Materials
Matériaux
Materialien

Colors
Couleurs
Farben

Capturing Space
Gain d'espace
Platz gewinnen

Distribution Distribution Aufteilung

Depending upon the available space and individual requirements, various types of layouts are possible. A built-in rectangular kitchen is recommended for long but small spaces. The L-shape design is based upon two contiguous walls while the U-shape allows three walls to be used and in so doing offers a great deal of work space. In the case of square rooms, a kitchen island in the middle of the room would be a sensible and comfortable alternative.

La place disponible et les besoins individuels seront déterminants dans les différents modes de distribution de l'espace. Une cuisine intégrée tout en longueur avantagera un espace restreint et long. L'agencement en forme de L nécessite deux murs attenants, alors que la distribution en fer à cheval se fera sur trois murs, offrant ainsi l'avantage d'un grand plan de travail. Dans une pièce carrée, l'idéal et le plus pratique est d'installer un îlot de cuisine au milieu de l'espace.

Je nach verfügbarem Platz und den individuellen Bedürfnissen der Benutzer sind unterschiedliche Arten der Raumaufteilung möglich. Eine geradlinige Küchenzeile ist bei sehr kleinen, länglichen Räumen vorteilhaft. Die Gestaltung in L-Form bedient sich zweier zusammenhängender Wände, während es die Aufteilung in U-Form erlaubt drei Wände zu nutzen und somit viel Arbeitsfläche bietet. Bei quadratischen Räumen ist eine Arbeitsinsel in der Mitte des Raumes eine sinnvolle und bequeme Alternative.

© Oscar Ferrari

© Pep Escoda

Lighting Eclairage Beleuchtung

In order to attain optimal illumination, the kitchen needs various light sources. If there is sufficient natural light, this should satisfy the main lighting requirements. Halogen lamps are a good supplement they create an effect very similar to natural light. The work and cooking areas require selective lighting that can be provided by fluorescent tubes or halogen lights under wall closets.

Afin d'obtenir un éclairage optimal, la cuisine nécessite plusieurs sources lumineuses. Si la lumière naturelle est suffisante, elle servira en grande partie d'éclairage principal. En complément, on peut choisir un spot halogène, dont la lumière claire se rapproche beaucoup de la lumière naturelle. Le plan de travail et de cuisine nécessitera un éclairage ponctuel, à l'instar d'un éclairage tubulaire ou de spots halogènes fixés sous les armoires murales.

Um eine optimale Ausleuchtung zu erzielen, benötigt die Küche verschiedene Lichtquellen. Ist ausreichend natürliches Licht vorhanden, sollte dieses weitestgehend genutzt werden. Als Ergänzung dazu sind Halogenstrahler eine gute Wahl, da sie ein der natürlichen Helligkeit sehr ähnliches Licht erzeugen. Der Arbeits- und Kochbereich benötigt darüber hinaus eine punktuelle Beleuchtung, die beispielsweise in Form von Leuchtstoffröhren oder Halogenstrahlern unter Hängeschränken befestigt werden kann.

Materials Matériaux Materialien

Flooring, wall coverings, furniture and work plates are manufactured in a wide range of materials and can be adapted to different spaces conditions and decorave styles. They must be extremely water- and heat- resistant and capable of being cleaned easily and quickly. Stainless steel, wood, stone, glass and various synthetic materials are most often used, as they all have the necessary attributes and are also attractive and decorative.

Revêtements du sol, habillage mural, meubles et plans de travail se déclinent dans une gamme de matériaux très variés, modulables selon l'espace et le style de décoration. Ils devront être hautement résistants à l'eau et à la chaleur et en outre faciles à nettoyer rapidement. Acier, bois, pierre et verre sans oublier toutes les variétés de matières synthétiques sont les matériaux les plus employés dans les modèles ci-joints : ils possèdent tous les avantages cités et sont, en outre, esthétiques et décoratifs.

Bodenbeläge, Wandverkleidungen, Möbel und Arbeitsplatten werden in vielfältigen Materialien hergestellt und können an unterschiedliche Raumverhältnisse und jeden Dekorationsstil angepasst werden. Sie müssen eine hohe Wasser- und Hitzeresistenz aufweisen und darüber hinaus leicht und schnell zu reinigen sein. Edelstahl, Holz, Stein, Glas sowie unterschiedliche Kunstoffe werden hier am häufigsten verwendet, da sie all diese Eigenschaften besitzen und zudem ästhetisch und dekorativ sind.

Stainless Steel Acier inoxydable Edelstahl

© Hideyuki Yamashita

© Artur G

Concrete Béton Zement

© José Luis Hausmann

Synthetic material Matières synthétiques Kunststoff

© Mark Guard

Natural Stone Pierre naturelle Naturstein

© Montse Garriga

Thanks to the development of new laminates and surface coverings, the color spectrum of today's kitchen is diverse and varied. The palette ranges from pastel colors such as beige, pale pink, light blue and pale yellow, to warm shades such as red, orange, sunny yellow and cooler colors like blue, green and gray. The general rule is that bright colors expand a room visually and are consequently particularly well-suited to small kitchens.

Grâce au développement de nouveaux laminés et de revêtements de surfaces, l'éventail des couleurs pour les cuisines est aujourd'hui riche et varié. Les teintes s'affichent dans une palette allant du beige, rose tendre, bleu clair et jaune pâle aux couleurs froides comme le bleu en passant par les nuances chaudes en rouge, orange et jaune vif, vert et gris. En règle générale, les couleurs vives, réputées pour agrandir l'espace, sont particulièrement indiquées pour les petites cuisines.

Durch die Entwicklung neuer Laminate und Oberflächenverkleidungen ist das Farbspektrum der Küche heutzutage vielseitig und abwechslungsreich. Die Palette reicht von Pastelltönen wie Beige, Zartrosa, Hellblau und Blassgelb über warme Schattierungen in Rot, Orange und Sonnengelb bis hin zu kalten Farben wie Blau, Grün und Grau. Generell gilt, dass helle und leuchtende Farben den Raum optisch vergrößern und deshalb für kleine Küchen besonders geeignet sind.

Green Vert Grün

© Miquel Tres

Blue Bleu Blau

Red Rouge Rot

Black Noir Schwarz

Capturing Space Gain d'espace Platz gewinnen

There are various ways of expanding a room optically. For one thing, depending upon the layout of the space available, clever placement of furniture can offer maximum surface area. So, for example, in an open space, a kitchen built into a wall can be combined with a work island, thereby adjoining room. Large windows, artificial light sources and pale colors reinforce the feeling of spaciousness.

Diverses possibilités sont offertes pour agrandir une petite pièce sur le plan optique. D'une part, selon le plan de l'espace disponible, il est possible de gagner un maximum de place en plaçant le mobilier judicieusement. Dans un espace ouvert, par exemple, on peut installer une cuisine intégrée contre le mur combinée à un îlot de cuisson, bénéficiant ainsi de l'espace restant. Grandes fenêtres, sources de lumière artificielle et couleurs claires exaltent la sensation d'espace.

Es gibt unterschiedliche Möglichkeiten, um bei kleinen Räumen einen optischen Vergrößerungseffekt zu erzielen. Je nach Grundriss des zur Verfügung stehenden Raumes Kann durch eine geschickte Platzierung der Möbel ein Maximum an Fläche gewonnen werden. So kann beispielsweise bei offenen Räumen eine an der Wand platzierte Küchenzeile mit einer Arbeitsinsel kombiniert werden, die vom übrigen Raum mitprofitiert. Große Fenster, künstliche Lichtquellen und helle Farbtöne verstärken darüber hinaus das Raumgefühl.

© Sergio Mah

© Paul Ratigan

Styles and Types
Styles et modèles
Stile und Typen

Kitchen styles and models are based upon a multitude of influences. The spectrum ranges from rustic Mediterranean country house models to high-tech stainless steel-coated professional kitchens. A decisive factor in the selection of a specific style is the taste and requirements of the user. As regards the specific kitchen model, today's market offers a variety of options that guarantee an attractive design as well as easy use and accessibility in even the smallest of surface areas. The kitchen concepts illustrated in this chapter range from open designs integrated into the living space to models with work islands to kitchens in which the cooking and eating spaces are merged.

Les styles de cuisine, à l'instar des modèles, sont soumis à diverses influences. L'éventail s'étend de la cuisine campagnarde, méditerranéenne et rustique haute en couleurs aux cuisines professionnelles tout en inox au design high-tech. Le choix du style se fera surtout en fonction des goûts et exigences de l'utilisateur. Le marché actuel offre, pour chaque modèle, les variantes les plus diverses, assurant même pour une surface limitée, un design esthétique et une utilisation facile. Les projets de cuisine vont des concepts intégrés à l'espace de vie, aux cuisines où la zone de cuisson et le coin repas font partie de la même pièce, en passant par les modèles intégrant des îlots de cuisson et de travail.

Küchenstile basieren ähnlich wie Modestile auf einer Vielzahl von Einflüssen. Das Spektrum reicht vom Farbenreichtum rustikal-mediterraner Landhausmodelle bis hin zum Hightech-Design edelstahlverkleideter Profiküchen. Ausschlaggebend für die Wahl einer bestimmten Stilrichtung ist allein der Geschmack und Anspruch des Benutzers. Was das jeweilige Küchenmodell betrifft, eröffnet der Markt heutzutage die unterschiedlichsten Möglichkeiten, die auch bei begrenzter Fläche ein ästhetisches Design sowie eine umkomplizierte Nutzung und Zugänglichkeit gewährleisten. Die in diesem Kapitel vorgestellten Küchenkonzepte reichen von offenen, in den Wohnraum integrierten Entwürfen über Modelle mit integrierter Koch- oder Arbeitsinsel bis hin zu Küchen, in denen sich Koch- und Essplatz in einem Raum befinden.

With a View
vec vue
Mit Aussicht

Avantgarde
Avant-gardiste
Avantgardistisch

Contemporary
Contemporain
Zeitgenössisch

Minimalist
Minimaliste
Minimalistisch

Maximalist
Maximaliste
Maximalistisch

Rustic
Rustique
Rustikal

Open Kitchens
Cuisines
ouvertes
Offene Küchen

Eat-in Kitchens
Cuisines
familiales
Wohnküchen

Kitchen Islands
Îlots de cuisson
Kochinseln

Compact Kitchens
Cuisines
compactes
Kompakte Küchen

With a view Avec vue Mit Aussicht

People for whom cooking means more than the simple warming up of prepared meals will opt for a kitchen with a view. With this concept, the user has the option of enjoying the surrounding landscape while preparing meals via a large glass window or doors.

Les cuisines avec vues s'adressent surtout à un public pour qui la cuisine ne s'arrête pas à réchauffer quelques plats pré cuisinés. Ce concept permet à son utilisateur de profiter de la vue panoramique à travers des baies ou des portes vitrées, tout en préparant leur repas.

Vor allem Personen, für die Kochen mehr bedeutet als nur das bloße Aufwärmen von Fertiggerichten, werden sich für eine Küche mit Aussicht entscheiden. Bei diesem Konzept hat der Benutzer die Möglichkeit, während der Zubereitung der Speisen, durch große Glasfenster oder Türen die Aussicht auf das umliegende Panorama zu geniessen.

© Massimo Iosa Ghini

Avantgarde Avant-gardiste Avantgardistisch

Avant-garde kitchens are characterized by a contemporary design and guarantee simple use and accessibility. Contrary to classic concepts, the individual areas are arranged independent of one another which results in a simpler and more dynamic total image. Materials such as stainless steel and wood are often combined with bright colors such as a saturated green or red.

Les cuisines avant-gardistes se caractérisent par un design contemporain tout en garantissant une utilisation pratique et simple. A l'inverse du concept classique, les différentes zones sont en grande partie agencées indépendamment les unes des autres, ce qui donne une vue d'ensemble plus légère et dynamique. Les matériaux, comme l'acier et le bois sont souvent combinés à des couleurs criardes, un vert intense ou du rouge.

Avantgardistische Küchen sind durch ein zeitgenössisches Design gekennzeichnet und garantieren eine unkomplizierte Nutzung und Zugänglichkeit. Im Gegensatz zu klassischen Konzepten sind hier die einzelnen Bereiche weitgehend unabhängig voneinander angeordnet, und das Gesamtbild wirkt dadurch leichter und dynamischer. Materialien wie Edelstahl und Holz werden oft mit grellen Farbtönen wie einem satten Grün oder Rot kombiniert.

Contemporary Contemporain Zeitgenössisch

Contemporary kitchens are characterized by solid and high-end design. Combinations of different materials such as wood, ceramic and synthetics give these kitchens a look of timeless elegance. Built-in cupboards and electronic appliances integrated into the furniture further guarantee optimal use of the available space.

Les cuisines contemporaines se définissent par un design solide et de qualité. Des associations de divers matériaux à l'instar du bois, de la céramique et des matières synthétiques confèrent à ces cuisines une allure d'élégance intemporelle. Meubles intégrés et appareils ménagers encastrés dans le mobilier garantissent en outre l'exploitation optimale de la place existante.

Zeitgenössische Küchen sind durch ein solides und hochwertiges Design gekennzeichnet. Kombinationen verschiedener Materialien wie Holz, Keramik und Kunststoff verleihen diesen Küchen einen Ausdruck zeitloser Eleganz. Einbauschränke und in das Mobiliar integrierte Elektrogeräte garantieren darüber hinaus eine optimale Ausnutzung des vorhandenen Platzes.

© Elmar Cucine

Minimalist Minimaliste Minimalistisch

Austerely designed and stylistically balanced, minimalist kitchens satisfy their decorative function via the principle of less is more. They are ideal for loft-style apartments as the design language of other spaces can be repeated in the kitchen. For this reason, they are often designed as open kitchens and can, as such, benefit from the light in the rest of the apartment.

Suivre une conception épurée et un style équilibré, telle est la fonction esthétique des cuisines minimalistes, suivant le principe moins c'est plus. Elles sont idéales pour les lofts ou pour les petits appartements où le langage formel des autres sphères de vie est repris par la cuisine. Elles sont souvent conçues comme des cuisines ouvertes, bénéficiant ainsi de la lumière de tout l'appartement.

Klar im Entwurf und stilistisch ausgewogen, erfüllen minimalistische Küchen ihre dekorative Funktion durch das Prinzip „less is more". Sie eignen sich optimal für Wohnungen im Loftstil oder kleine Appartements, in denen die Formsprache anderer Wohnungsbereiche durch die Küche wieder aufgenommen wird. Häufig werden sie deshalb als offene Küchen entworfen und können somit von dem Licht der übrigen Wohnung profitieren.

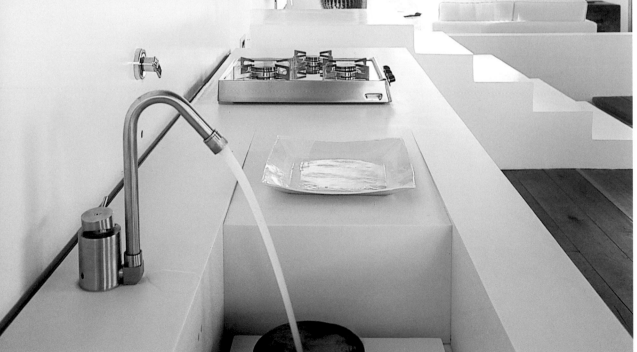

© Hertha Hurnaus

Maximalist Maximaliste Maximalistisch

A combination of the aesthetic of the 18th and 19th centuries with elements of the 50s, 60s and 70s is characteristic of the maximalist style. This kitchen concept is rarely limited to a single material - often stainless steel and wood are combined with colorful ceramic tiles. Maximalist kitchens feature colorful accessories and small household appliances that are stored in view and thereby serve as additional decorative elements.

Le style maximaliste se définit par un mélange d'esthétiques du XVIIIe et du XIXe siècles et d'éléments des années cinquante, soixante et soixante-dix. Ce concept de cuisine se limite rarement à l'emploi d'un matériau, mais utilise davantage des alliances d'inox et de bois avec des carreaux de céramique colorés. Ce qui frappe dans les cuisines maximalistes, c'est l'abondance d'accessoires colorés et de petits appareils ménagers qui, en guise de rangement, sont exposés, servant aussi d'objets de décoration.

Kennzeichnend für den maximalistischen Stil ist eine Kombination der Ästhetik des 18. und 19. Jahrhunderts mit Elementen der 50er, 60er und 70er Jahre. Bei diesem Küchenkonzept beschränkt man sich nur selten auf ein Material - häufig werden Edelstahl und Holz zusammen mit bunten Keramikfliesen verwendet. Auffallend bei maximalistischen Küchen ist eine Fülle an buntem Zubehör und kleinen Haushaltsgeräten, die sichtbar aufbewahrt werden und somit als zusätzliche Dekorationselemente dienen.

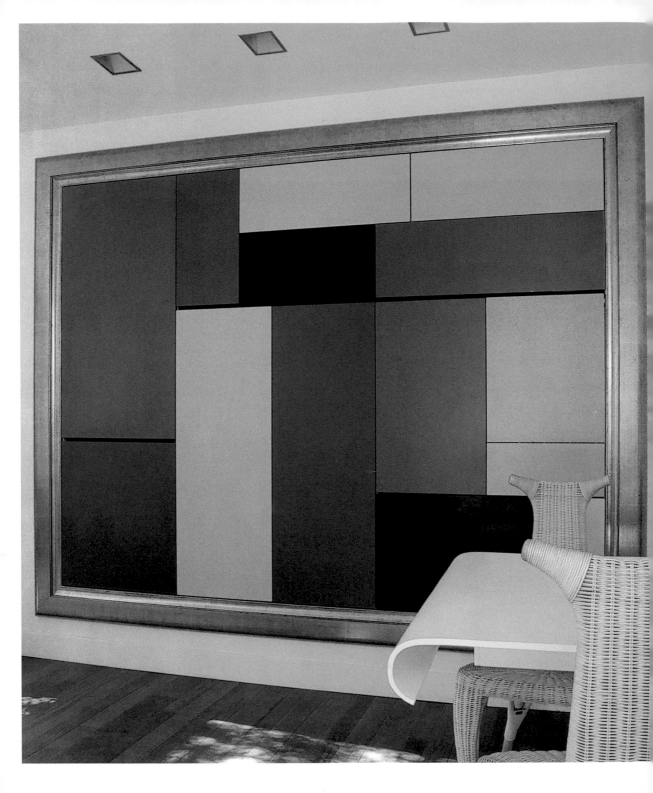

© Eugeni Pons

Rustic Rustique Rustikal

This chapter presents kitchens that embody a lifestyle close to nature and the countryside. Furnishings and fixtures made of unprocessed solid wood and stone are used. In order to create a Mediterranean style, elements in blue, white or green colors are recommended, along with decoration with clay jugs, meadow flowers and dried herbs.

Ce chapitre présente les cuisines qui incarnent un style de vie près de la nature et de la campagne. On préférera ici un mobilier et des robinetteries en bois massif et pierre. Pour créer un style méditerranéen, on favorisera les éléments déclinant des tons dans les blanc, bleu ou vert, auxquels seront associés des cruches en terre décorées de fleurs des champs et herbes séchées.

In diesem Kapitel werden Küchen vorgestellt, die einen ländlichen und natürlichen Lebensstil verkörpern. So werden hier bevorzugt Mobiliar und Armaturen aus naturbelassenem Massivholz und Stein verwendet. Um einen mediterranen Stil zu kreieren, empfiehlt sich die Verwendung von Elementen in blauen, weißen oder grünen Farbtönen, die beispielsweise mit Tonkrügen, Wiesenblumen und Trockenkräutern dekoriert werden können.

© Montse Garriga

Open Kitchens Cuisines ouvertes Offene Küchen

Ever since new appliances and ventilation systems have been enssuring that smells and steam do not travel to the neighboring living area, open kitchens integrated into the living space have become increasingly popular. Apart from their space-saving characteristics, these kitchens also offer the advantage that the eating area - often separated visually only by a table with bar stools - may be directly connected to the kitchen.

Depuis la création de nouveaux appareils et systèmes d'aération pour empêcher la diffusion de vapeurs et d'odeurs dans le reste de l'appartement, l'engouement pour les cuisines ouvertes, intégrées à l'espace de vie, ne cesse de croître. En dehors du gain d'espace qu'elles représentent, ces cuisines offrent aussi l'avantage d'établir une liaison directe entre la cuisine et le coin repas, que seuls une table et des tabourets de bar séparent.

Seitdem neue Geräte und Belüftungssysteme dafür sorgen, dass Gerüche und Dampf sich nicht im übrigen Wohnraum verteilen, ist die Beliebtheit offener, in den Raum integrierter Küchen gestiegen. Abgesehen von ihrer platzsparenden Eigenschaft, bieten diese Küchen zudem den Vorteil, dass der Essbereich, der oftmals optisch nur durch eine Tischplatte mit Barhockern abgegrenzt ist, direkt mit der Küche verbunden werden kann.

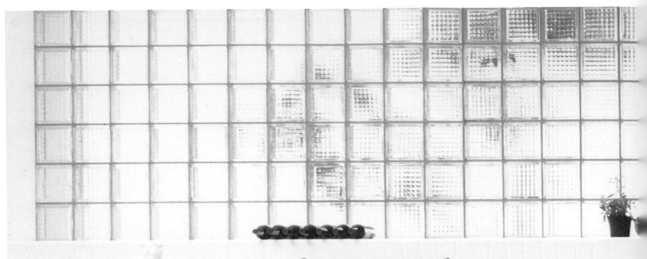

Eat-in Kitchens   Cuisines familiales   Wohnküchen

In eat-in kitchens, which originate from the concept of old farmhouses, the cooking and eating areas are located in a room. This does not have to mean, however, that residential kitchens always require a great deal of space. If only limited space is available, the eating area may either assume the form of a bar with stools or an open design with a table and chairs that spill over on to the remaining living area.

Les cuisines familiales, issues du concept d'anciennes pièces de fermes, réunissent la zone de cuisine et la salle à manger en une seule pièce. Cela ne signifie pas pour autant que les grandes cuisines prennent toujours beaucoup de place. Si l'espace offert est restreint, le coin repas peut être créé soit par un bar doté de tabourets, ou selon un concept ouvert, intégré avec une table et des chaises à l'espace de vie attenant.

In Wohnküchen, die aus dem Konzept ehemaliger Bauernstuben hervorgehen, befinden sich Koch- und Essplatz in einem Raum. Das muss jedoch nicht zwangsläufig bedeuten, dass Wohnküchen stets eine große Fläche vorraussetzen. Ist nur wenig Platz vorhanden, kann der Essplatz entweder in Form einer Bar mit Barhockern gestaltet werden, oder auch als offener Entwurf mit einem Tisch und Stühlen, die in den übrigen Wohnbereich übergehen.

© Montse Garriga

136

© Jordi Miralles

© Mihail Moldeoveanu

Kitchen Islands Îlots de cuisson Kochinseln

If only limited space is available, a cooking or working island is usually established in kitchens integrated into the living area. The characteristics of this type of island concept is an element which can be accessed from all sides and which includes both the cooking area as well as a sink or work area.

Si la surface disponible est très limitée, un îlot de cuisson ou de travail sera intégré à la cuisine ouverte sur l'espace de vie. Un tel concept d'îlot se définit par un élément accessible de tous côtés et qui contient à côté des plaques de cuisson, un évier ou un plan de travail.

Ist nur eine begrenzte Fläche vorhanden, wird eine Koch- oder Arbeitsinsel vor allem bei offenen, in den Wohnraum integrierten Küchen eingesetzt. Das Charakteristische eines solchen Inselkonzepts ist ein Element, das von allen Seiten frei zugänglich ist und das sowohl die Kochstelle als auch eine Spüle oder Arbeitsfläche beinhaltet.

© René Chavanne

Compact Kitchens Cuisines compactes Kompakte Küchen

If space requirements are at a minimum, compact kitchens often offer the perfect solution. They are usually made up of a unit containing appliances for cooling, cooking, washing dishes, as well as a work area that uses the remaining area for storage. Other concepts provide for individual, independent modules that cover sinks and cooking areas when not in use so that they may be used for other purposes.

Les cuisines compactes sont souvent la solution idéale face à des conditions spatiales réduites au minimum. La plupart du temps, il s'agit d'un bloc cuisine contenant les éléments de réfrigération, cuisson, vaisselle et plan de travail y compris un espace de rangement. D'autres concepts prévoient des modules indépendants les uns des autres, où évier et zone de cuisson sont recouverts lorsqu'ils ne sont pas utilisés, pour servir de plan de travail.

Sind die räumlichen Vorraussetzungen auf ein Minimum begrenzt, bieten kompakte Küchen oftmals eine optimale Lösung. Meistens bestehen sie aus einem zusammenhängenden Element, das Kühl- Koch-, Spül- und Arbeitsbereich integriert und bei dem die übrige Fläche als Stauram dient. Andere Konzepte sehen einzelne, voneinander unabhängige Module vor, bei denen Spüle und Kochstelle bei Nichtgebrauch abgedeckt, und für andere Zwecke genutzt werden können.

© Berloni Cucine

Electric Appliances and Accessories
Appareils électriques et accessoires
Elektrogeräte und Zubehörteile

Electronic appliances in the kitchen are often integrated into the furniture. Here the design either focuses on a specific color scheme or a mix of styles in which materials such as wood and chrome are combined with each other. Technical innovations have allowed stoves and refrigerators to not only be used as built-in appliances but also as freestanding individual elements. Influences of various cultures from all over the world have allowed kitchens to be enriched with a large number of appliances, such as woks, steam pots and sandwich makers. In addition to their specific function, these also serve as decorative design objects.

Les appareils électriques d'une cuisine sont souvent intégrés dans le mobilier. Le design offre un éventail allant d'une gamme de couleurs déterminée à un mélange de styles, où des matériaux comme le bois, le chrome se marient entre eux. Grâce aux innovations technologiques, fours et réfrigérateurs ne sont plus uniquement des éléments intégrés mais aussi des unités indépendantes. Les influences de cultures du monde entier transforment l'univers de la cuisine, enrichis d'appareils tels que woks, cocotte-minute ou machines à sandwich. A leur fonction s'ajoute l'esthétique, les métamorphosant en objets design.

Die Elektrogeräte einer Küche werden häufig in das Mobiliar integriert. Hierbei bewegt sich das Design entweder in einem ausgewählten Farbspektrum oder es kommt zu einem Stilmix, indem Materialien wie etwa Holz und Chrom miteinander kombiniert werden. Technische Innovationen haben dazu beigetragen, dass Herde und Kühlschränke nicht nur als Einbaugeräte verwendet werden, sondern auch als freistehende Einzelelemente zum Einsatz kommen. Einflüsse unterschiedlicher Kulturen aus der ganzen Welt haben dazu geführt, dass die Küchen um eine Vielzahl an Küchengeräten wie Woks, Dampfkochtöpfe oder Sandwichmaker bereichert wurden. Diese dienen neben ihrer reinen Funktion auch als dekorative Designobjekte.

Store and Hang
Entreposer et ranger
Lagern und Aufbewahren

Cook and Bake
Cuisiner et cuire au four
Kochen und Backen

Cool and Freeze
Refroidir et congeler
Kühlen und Gefrieren

Ventilate
Aérer
Lüften

Wash and Clean
Laver et nettoyer
Abwaschen und Spülen

Accessories
Accessoires
Zubehör

© Alno

Store and Hang Entreposer et ranger Lagern und Aufbewahren

A kitchen's storage space should be planned around the three main areas of sink, cooking area and larder. Upper and lower cupboards are especially well-suited to small rooms. In this way, the space under the work areas can also be used optimally. Rods and rails serve as practical and decorative accessories that can be added to the front of a kitchen or hang from the ceiling.

L'espace rangement d'une cuisine doit être planifié autour de trois domaines principaux évier, cuisson et placard à provisions. Le système de placards accrochés et posés est parfait dans les petites pièces, donnant la possibilité d'optimaliser l'espace sous le plan de travail. Les accessoires, tels que tiges et rails, à la fois pratiques et décoratifs, sont installés sur la façade de la cuisine ou descendent du plafond.

Der Stauraum in einer Küche sollte rund um die drei Hauptbereiche Spüle, Kochbereich und Speiseschrank geplant werden. Ober- und Unterschränke eignen sich vor allem für kleine Räume, da so auch der Platz um die Arbeitsflächen herum optimal genutzt werden kann. Als praktische und dekorative Zubehörteile dienen zudem Stangen und Schienen, die an der Küchenfront angebracht werden oder von der Decke herabhängen.

© Alno

174

© Alno

Cook and Bake Cuisiner et cuire au four Kochen und Backen

The choice of an electric or gas stove depends upon the individual needs of the user. A combination of both systems is very popular nowadays. Modern Ceran cooking surfaces also offer the advantage of speeding up the cooking process and also feature new designs.

Le choix d'une cuisinière à gaz ou électrique dépend des besoins individuels de l'utilisateur. La combinaison des deux systèmes est très en vogue actuellement. Les plans de cuisson modernes en vitrocéramique offrent l'avantage, d'une part, d'accélérer le processus de cuisson et d'autre part de se décliner dans une gamme de designs innovants.

Ob die Wahl auf einen Elektro- oder einen Gasherd fällt, hängt von den individuellen Bedürfnissen des Benutzers ab. Sehr beliebt ist heute auch eine Kombination aus beiden Systemen. Moderne Cerankochfelder bieten darüber hinaus den Vorteil, dass sie einerseits den Kochvorgang beschleunigen und zudem neuartige Designs aufweisen.

Cool and Freeze Refroidir et congeler Kühlen und Gefrieren

In the area of refrigerators, the industry has made spectacular innovations over the past few years. So-called smart refrigerators with a touch screen integrated in the door allow for the control of stored foodstuffs. As regards design, the palette ranges from the Retrolook model in explosive colors to a transparent example made of steel and glass.

Dans le secteur de la réfrigération, l'industrie a été traversée, au cours de ces dernières années, par un courant innovateur spectaculaire. Les réfrigérateurs appelés intelligents, dotés d'une touche électronique intégrée dans la porte, peuvent contrôler les aliments qu'ils contiennent. Pour ce qui est du design, la palette va du modèle au look rétro dans des couleurs explosives aux exemplaires tout en transparence, à base d'acier et de verre.

Auf dem Gebiet der Kühlschränke hat die Industrie in den letzten Jahren eine Vielzahl spektakulärer Neuerungen hervorgebracht. So genannte intelligente Kühlschränke mit einem in der Kühlschranktüre integrierten "Touch screen" ermöglichen die Kontrolle der eingelagerten Lebensmittel. Was das Design betrifft, reicht die Palette vom "Retrolook" Modell in explosiven Farben bis hin zum transparenten Exemplar aus Stahl und Glas.

Ventilate Aérer Lüften

These days, extractor hoods are quiet, powerful and energy-saving. They are often made of rust-free steel and most models also have built-in halogen radiators. Appliances with swivel arms that suction off steam and smells at source also function as a decorative element.

De nos jours, les hottes aspirantes sont silencieuses, puissantes et consomment peu d'énergie. La plupart du temps en inox, la majorité des modèles sont dotés de spots halogènes. Les appareils à orientation pivotante, permettant d'absorber vapeurs et odeurs en un lieu précis, se transforment en éléments décoratifs qui accrochent le regard.

Dunstabzugshauben sind heutzutage leise, leistungsstark und energiesparend. Häufig werden sie aus rostfreiem Stahl hergestellt und die meisten Modelle verfügen über eingebaute Halogenstrahler. Geräte mit Schwenkarm, die das Absaugen von Dämpfen und Gerüchen direkt am Entstehungsort ermöglichen, dienen darüber hinaus als dekorativer Blickfang.

Wash and Clean Laver et nettoyer Abwaschen und Spülen

A decisive factor for the selection of sinks is the available space as well as the number of required basins. The material should be suited to the style of the kitchen. In order to maximize the available space, the latest designs offer a combination of basins and rinsing areas, which may be covered when not in use and thereby serve as additional work space.

Le choix de l'évier est déterminé par la place disponible et par le nombre de bacs nécessaires. Le matériel doit également correspondre au style de la cuisine. Pour optimaliser la place disponible, les designs les plus innovants prévoient de combiner évier et zone d'égouttage. Lorsqu'elle n'est pas utilisée, cette zone peut être recouverte, augmentant ainsi le plan de travail.

Maßgeblich für die Wahl der Spüle sind der verfügbare Platz sowie die Anzahl der erforderlichen Becken. Das Material sollte hierbei an den Stil der Küche angepasst werden. Um den vorhandenen Platz optimal auszunutzen, sehen neuste Designs eine Kombination aus Becken und Abtropffläche vor, die bei Nichtbenutzung abgedeckt werden können, und sicht somit in eine zur zusätzlichen Arbeitsfläche verwandeln.

© Alno

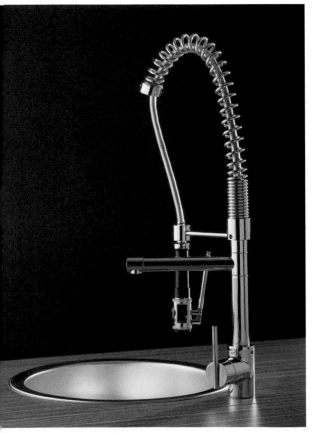

© Alno

© Alno

Accessories Accessoires Zubehör

A plethora of utensils simplifies the preparation of meals and accessories such as tea kettles, coffee machines and toasters may be found in almost every kitchen. In addition to their function, these objects offer a highly decorative function and can substantially impact the total style of the kitchen with their color.

Une foule d'ustensiles simplifie la préparation et la cuisson de plats. Les accessoires, à l'instar de bouilloire et cafetière électriques et de toasters font presque toujours partie de la batterie de cuisine. Ces objets ne sont pas uniquement fonctionnels mais aussi hautement décoratifs et leur coloris peut influencer tout le style de la cuisine.

Eine Fülle an Utensilien, die das Vorbereiten und Kochen von Speisen vereinfachen, wie zum Beispiel Teekessel, Kaffeemaschinen und Toaster, sind in nahezu jeder Küche zu finden. Neben ihrer Funktion haben diese Objekte eine höchst dekorative Aufgabe und können mit entsprechender Farbgebung den Gesamtstil der Küche entscheidend beeinflussen.

Special thanks to Remerciements particuliers à Mit besonderem Dank an

AEM
Alessi
Alfons Soldevila
Alno
Animal Design Factory
Antonio Obrador/Estudio Denario
Arteks
Ayhan Ozan/AIA
Blockarchitecture
Brian Housden
Bruno Raymond
Bryan MacKay-Lyons
Bulthaup
Carlos Mir
Chalon
Chavanne & Holzer Design
Christopher Ash, James Soane/Project Orange
David Salmela
Designkoop
Disaster Design
Eichinger oder Knechel
Elena Calderón
Elmar Cucine
Estrella Salietti
Estudio GCA
Estudio Olatz de Ituarte
Fátima Vilaseca
Feyferlik-Fritzer
Fletcher Roger Associates
Guillermo Arias
Hecker Phelan Pty. Ltd.
Héctor Restrepo Calvo/Heres Arquitectura
Heinz Hellermann
Hideyuki Yamashita
Inês Lobo
JAM Design
Javier Sol, Juan Manuel Fernández, Ana López/OTO Estudio
Jeffrey McKean
Joan Bach

Jonathan Clark
Jordi Sarrà
Josep Juvé
Juerg Meister
Karl and Lesley Lawton
Kurt Lichtblau/Konrad Spindler Architekten
Marble Fairbanks Architects
Marcelo Gizzarelli, Mercedes Sanguinetti
Massimo Iosa Ghini
Mauro Pelizzari
Messana O'Rorke Architects
Michael Graves & Associates for Target
Moneo Brock Studio
Mutsue Hayakusa/Cell Space Architects
Nardi Architecture
Niall McLaughlin
Nimrod Setter
Original Vision Limited
Pablo Fernández Lorenzo, Pablo Redondo Díez
Peanutz Architekten
Pool Architektur
Propeller Z
Ramón Berga
Ruhl Walker
Sandra Aparicio, Ignacio Forteza
Satoshi Okada Architects
Siemens
Simon Platt, Rob Dubois
Smeg
Surface Architects
Takao Shiotsuka Atelier
Target
Teresa Sepulcre
Tom McCallum, Shania Shegedyn
Tow Studios
Villeroy & Boch
Vincent van Duysen Architects
Wespi, De Meuron
Whirlpool